I0148739

Charles Albert Catlin

Baking Powders

A Treatise of the Character, Methods for the Determination of the Values,

etc.

Charles Albert Catlin

Baking Powders
A Treatise of the Character, Methods for the Determination of the Values, etc.

ISBN/EAN: 9783744743914

Printed in Europe, USA, Canada, Australia, Japan

Cover: Foto ©ninafisch / pixelio.de

More available books at **www.hansebooks.com**

BAKING POWDERS.

A TREATISE ON THEIR CHARACTER, METHODS FOR
THE DETERMINATION OF THEIR VALUES, ETC.

WITH SPECIAL REFERENCE TO

RECENT IMPROVEMENTS IN PHOSPHATE POWDERS.

BY

CHARLES A. CATLIN, B. S., Ph.B., F. A. A. A. S.

PUBLISHED BY THE
RUMFORD CHEMICAL WORKS,
PROVIDENCE, R. I., U.S.A.
1899.

CONTENTS.

ILLUSTRATIONS.

PHOTO-MICROGRAPHS OF THE CONSTITUENTS OF RUMFORD BAKING POWDER.

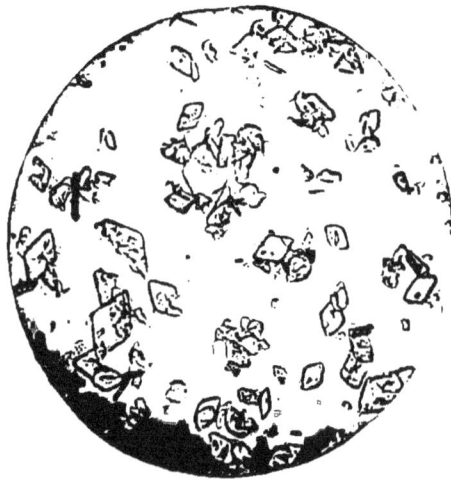

Crystals of Bicarbonate of Sodium, the source of the leavening carbon dioxide gas in Rumford Baking Powder.

Pure Corn Starch.

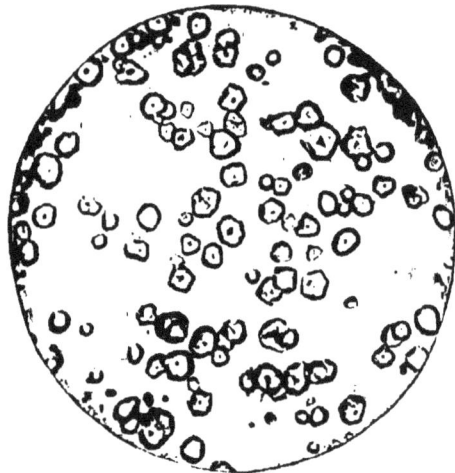

Crystals of Monocalcium Phosphate, which, in admixture with starch, forms the active acid agent in Rumford Baking Powder.

6

Baking Powders.

Hygienic Quality.

Baking Powders have for their essential constituents, sodium bicarbonate and some form of acid or acid salt. During the bread making process in which they are employed, under the influence of the water or other liquid used in mixing the dough, chemical reaction more or less complete ensues between these constituents, resulting in the evolution of the leavening carbon dioxide gas, which is eventually dissipated, and a fixed residue, saline for the most part, which remains. It is, therefore, the character of this residue which determines the hygienic quality of any baking powder.

Based upon these residues, Baking Powders may be conveniently divided into three well defined groups:

1st. Baking Powders conveying to the food in which they are used, a saline addition of phosphates, for the most part of calcium and sodium.

2nd. Baking Powders conveying to the food in which they are used, a saline addition of tartrates, for the most part potassium-sodium tartrate, more commonly known as the medicine Rochelle salt.

3rd. Baking Powders conveying to the food in which they are used, a saline addition of sodium sulphate, more commonly known as the medicine Glauber's salt, and an aluminum salt, or aluminum hydrate, or both, as the case may be.

Considering the hygienic quality of powders of the various classes, we find in the first, the residue left in the food is wholly composed of phosphates, of calcium and sodium for the greater part; and that these phosphates are normal constituents of both animal and vegetable food. Furthermore, we find careful research has demonstrated animal life cannot exist without a supply of these phosphates; since they not only go to make up an important element of bodily structure, but play an essential part as well in the process of bodily nutrition.

It has been proved by research, in all the higher forms of animal life, if not in every form of animal life without exception, there is a demand for a constant supply of these phosphates and a corresponding constant waste through their utilization in the life process; and that the organs of the animal body are specially constructed for the continued elimination of these phosphate wastes without injury, or even the slightest disturbance of any of their functions.

These phosphate baking powders are in fact the sole exemplification of leavening agents which do not introduce, as a residuum of their action, material abnormal to food; and are further unique, in that their residues, in and of themselves, contribute essential salts in form available to the animal economy.

Considering the hygienic quality of powders of the second class, wherein potassium-sodium tartrate is the saline residue, we find this salt, while possessing medicinal and remedial value under certain disturbed conditions of health, is never present as a normal constituent of the animal body, nor yet as a normal constituent of food of any kind; neither does it in itself possess nutritious value, nor contribute nutrient qualities to food in which it may be present, nor yet assist in any degree the digestive function. The use of baking powders, from which it is the resultant, is, in fact, defended by interested parties, only upon claims for the innoxiousness of the residue, based, to say the least, upon very questionable data. Hygienic qualities are never claimed for it, except when it shall have undergone a supposable change of condition. This change of condition by a most ingenious distortion of fact they claim possible, through the operation of certain obscure physiological influences decomposing the objectionable tartrate to carbonates; which, in some mysterious way, sufficient phosphate being present in the food, react to become phosphates; when all the virtues, and only the virtues of phosphates are claimed for the resultant. When it is considered that such decomposition of a salt, if it ever takes place, involves consumption of energy in the operation, it certainly is questionable whether the phosphate derived by such roundabout process has not cost the animal economy more than it will ever receive in return; especially when one realizes that the phosphates of the food were probably directly available without it. If it remains as Rochelle salt it is certainly an open question whether it be innoxious. Physiologists have determined, while this salt in doses of one-half to one ounce is an active cathartic, in smaller doses it is absorbed by the system and renders the urine alkaline. A most dangerous condition if prolonged, and one certainly not to be invited by the continued ingestion of the salt in ones daily food. In fact, the dangers would seem to be even greater from the small doses taken in bread raised with powders of this class than from the larger cathartic doses.

In some cases, powders of this class, being prepared by the employment of a portion of free tartaric acid, leave as an element of their saline residue, sodium tartrate, a salt quite as objectionable as the Rochelle salt, with no hygienic qualities whatever to recommend it.

Summing up then the qualities of this second class of powders, we cannot but be led to the conclusion, that their employment in food is, to say the least, decidedly *unhygienic.*

The hygienic quality of powders of the third class, commonly called "Alum" powders (or "Alum-Phosphate" when a little phosphate is added) wherein the residue of their operation consists of sodium sulphate and aluminum hydrate, or an aluminum salt like the basic sulphate or the phosphate, is certainly questionable. Sodium sulphate, commonly known as Glauber's salt, like Rochelle salt, is an active cathartic in doses of one-half to one ounce, but of much less injurious possibilities when taken in smaller doses long continued, being really a normal excretion of the body. But its nauseous taste gives it a most objectionable quality in bread making. It may therefore be called a harmless though undesirable resultant. Not so of the aluminum constituent of the residue from this class of powders, the presence of which is, without doubt, exceedingly dangerous in food, especially in that of invalids or of persons having weak digestive powers. It is claimed by interested parties, that when a phosphate is used in connection with the aluminum salt in the composition of these powders, the residue of the operation in food is an insoluble, and consequently harmless, aluminum phosphate. Facts however do not seem to prove that aluminum phosphate is insoluble in the juices of the stomach. And furthermore, extended investigation shows that when phosphate addition has been made to baking powders having an aluminum salt for their active acid ingredient, it is never in anywhere near the required proportion to combine with all the aluminum present. The real purpose of its addition being to give a quick acting property to the powder, which it lacks when the aluminum salt alone is employed as the acid agent, and not to supply the phosphate for the reaction to aluminum phosphate, nor yet because of its hygienic quality. It is further true, that in baking powders where alum or aluminum sulphate is the active acid agent, especially if it be in the dried anhydrous condition, the reactions of the baking process are liable to be incomplete, and basic aluminum sulphate result, which cannot be other than a dangerous addition to food. Chemical and physiological literature teems with testimony to the exceedingly baneful results following the administration of soluble aluminum salts of any kind. In regard to aluminum hydrate there is a large amount of testimony from high authorities, all to the effect that it acts to retard digestion, if not wholly to arrest it; that it enters into insoluble combination with valuable constituents of food to render them unavailable, especially the albuminoids and phosphates; beside having an irritant and highly astringent effect upon the mucous membrane of the alimentary canal; while some assert, that it produces a most disastrous effect upon the nervous system.

Leavening Quality.

Of course the hygienic quality of a baking powder is of first importance, but for its designed purpose there are other qualities which determine its value.

It is perfectly understood, that the object of any leavening process is to impart a light cellular structure to the finished loaf or cake; and that this is effected generally by in some way evolving carbon dioxide within the dough, in proper quantity, and at the proper stage of the cooking or baking operation. Baking powders are means to this end; and for their true valuation a clear understanding of the cooking or baking process is necessary.

In an article published in the Journal of Analytical Chemistry, Vol. IV, Page 361, October, 1890, I gave details of some investigations of mine upon the conditions of the baking process, which will be useful to us in this connection. From this I quote:

"To inform myself more exactly, I made many careful observations of the steps pursued by a cook of the best homespun order, in preparation of baking powder biscuit dough and subsequent baking of the same. I found that she was using about 504 gms. of flour (Haxall brand) for the quart, as leavening for which two heaping teaspoonfuls of a popular brand of baking powder, weighing together about 17 gms., and for moistening, 386 gms. of either milk or water, or about 23 cc. of liquid for each gram of baking powder employed.

The range of temperature and the length of exposure thereto, were noted as follows: When the dough was ready for baking, a thermometer was inserted so that the bulb might be held as near as possible at the centre of the biscuit or loaf, and the whole placed in the already heated oven by the cook in the usual manner, the range of temperature being observed through a peephole, and record made thereof at stated times.

Averaging a series of accordant results thus obtained, I found the oven at the outset to have a temperature of about 380° F., and that the temperature of the interior of the dough passed through the following range:

After	1	minute's	exposure	in	the	oven	95° F.
"	3	"	"	"	"	"	130° "
"	4	"	"	"	"	"	150° "
"	5	"	"	"	"	"	160° "
"	7	"	"	· "	"	"	205° "
"	10	"	"	"	"	"	205° "
"	12	"	"	"	"	"	210° "
"	13	"	"	"	"	"	212° "
"	15	"	"	"	"	"	212° "
"	17	"	"	"	"	"	217° "

After thirteen minutes exposure, the cook pronounced the biscuit "done"; but for the sake of the experiment, the heating was continued, when, after fifteen minutes, the crust had become far too brown to be palatable, while at the end of seventeen, actual burning had well commenced. From the above it is apparent then, that in the actual baking process, the temperature of the dough is raised gradually, through a lapse of about thirteen minutes, to a temperature of not more than 212° F., and for a successful issue this should not endure for more than one minute, if indeed it should be allowed to continue for that length of time."

In the first place, all ordinary operations of the kitchen, if graduated at all, are by measure and not by weight. The quart of flour demands the two or three teaspoonfuls of baking powder, always measured, never weighed. It has been found that somewhere about 68 cubic inches of carbon dioxide gas is the proper volume to raise 1 quart of flour, loosely packed (1 lb.); or a little less than a volume and a quarter of gas to one volume of the flour for ordinary biscuit or bread. Very much less than this gives poor results; while very much more is practically of no value. Stating this another way: Experience has taught that in domestic use a powder properly evolving 50 times its own volume of gas is about the right standard. The available gas-evolving power of a baking powder to meet the common domestic requirements should then be somewhere about 50 to 60 times that of its own volume. That is to say, a baking powder should have a volumetric leavening or aerating coefficient of 50 to 60. This is indeed a very important question in determining the value of a baking powder, which is not a question of percentage by weight, but one wholly of percentage by volume. For it is readily seen, that as much leavening value may be obtained in domestic use from the same volume of powder purchased, in one having a low percentage of carbon dioxide with high density, as from one having high percentage of carbon dioxide with low density. Therefore, the true measure of efficiency of a baking powder is one dependent upon volumetric considerations, and not one of percentage by weight, as is usually reported.

But this available carbon dioxide does not tell the whole story of baking powder valuation by any means. It is almost as important to know the manner of its evolution as it is to know its total volume. When one considers the dough mixing process it is easily understood, if a baking powder be employed which gives a too prompt reaction, much of the leavening gas will be evolved and lost in the manipulation, especially if the dough be rolled and handled. In thin batter, like griddle cake batter, especially where considerable time necessarily elapses between the mixing and the cooking, this quick cold evolution is a matter of serious importance.

It is manifest also, on the other hand, that a baking powder too tardy in character, requiring a high oven temperature to bring about reaction, cannot give good results. When such baking powder is used, the dough placed in the hot oven is speedily crusted over, long before the interior of the loaf has attained the reacting temperature, and the mass of the dough itself under the oven influence has become considerably solidified as well. When now the exciting temperature is attained, the reaction ensues with almost explosive violence, producing a result that is anything but the delicate cellular structure desired. The conditions under which the evolution of the gas takes place is, therefore, a most important consideration in the valuation of a baking powder.

It is plain that a baking powder evolving its carbon dioxide quite gradually from the first of the mixing process and on into the oven, not so tardy as to require the extreme heat of the baking process, nor yet so active as to expend itself entirely by the cold evolution, is the ideal. To measure this quality of a baking powder, is really a very difficult matter. A useful determination indicating something in this direction is that of the amount of carbon dioxide given off simply in the cold, when treated with the quantity of water used in mixing the dough.

The question of the amount of water to be used to fairly represent the conditions of the baking process is one of some moment. Referring again to my investigation of the conditions of the baking process: In actual process we found that 23 cc. of water were employed for each gram of baking powder. A large part of this water, being absorbed by the flour, must have been practically inert in bringing about reaction between the constituents of the powder. Just what this absorbed water would be, we have not the means of determining; but certainly, not more than half the water employed can be considered as exerting solvent action upon the powder. I would therefore recommend that not more than 10 cc. be used for each gram of baking powder taken in making the determination. This amount of water, of course, also represents that necessary to imitate the whole baking process, oven operations and all.

In the oven baking, however, the further elements of temperature and time come in for consideration. Referring again, on this point, to my investigation: We found in our observations of the baking of the biscuit, that in the matter of temperature, 212° F. was never exceeded within the dough in proper manipulation, and that this limit should never be allowed to endure for more than one minute at the longest. As a matter of fact, I believe that when the temperature reaches 200° F., or even at a much lower point, the dough has attained such consistency that further evolution of gas is rather an injury than an advantage. However this may be, it is certain that gas evolved beyond the limit of a temperature of 212° F., enduring for one minute, is of no practical value.

Upon the operation of the baking process as observed, fixing the conditions of moisture, time of cold evolution, time of heating, etc., I have based the methods for the valuation of baking powders described in the context.

As I have said, this matter of extra-oven, or cold-evolution, of the carbon dioxide of a baking powder, is one of great importance; and one to which the manufacturer should be keenly alert. To adjust this ratio between the total available and the cold carbon dioxide to greatest efficiency for all kinds of baking work, would be out of the question; for this would demand

for cake one ratio, for biscuit another, for griddle cakes
another, etc.   Thus this adjustment becomes a matter
of judgment as to average efficiency in the baking
operations of the household.

A ratio somewhere between 60 and 70 for this cold, to
the 100 available carbon dioxide, seems to best meet
the popular favor, and is about the ratio adopted for
the better class of powders.

Recent Improvements in Phosphate Powders.

The peculiar value of acid calcium phosphates in
healthfulness and efficiency, was early appreciated by
Professor Horsford, who first suggested their use and
invented processes for their manufacture in suitable form
for culinary purposes.   But there was one quality of
these acidulated phosphates, as he was then only able to
prepare them, which for many years seemed to forbid
their successful employment as active acid components
of baking powders to be packed in unsealed cans.   This
was in their powerful avidity for moisture, or deliques-
cent property; which, it is readily understood, would
be fatal, in unsealed packages, to any reasonable commercial stability.   But years of patient research was at
length rewarded by the discovery of a process through
which, to the surprise of everyone who had been
familiar with past efforts, a baking powder composed
only of monocalcium phosphate, sodium bicarbonate
and starch, might be prepared, which was even supe-
rior to potassium bitartrate baking powders in the
quality of commercial stability.   The valuable qualities
of the new discovery were soon turned to practical

account in preparing the powder now sold under the name of Rumford Baking Powder, made by the Rumford Chemical Works, of Providence, R. I., the original manufacturers under Professor Horsford's patents and with whom he was identified. This baking powder is composed of pure monobasic orthophosphates, mostly of calcium with the usual small traces of magnesium, sodium and iron, pure sodium bicarbonate and pure corn starch. These, by peculiar processes of manipulation, are so brought together into admixture as to form a baking powder having commercial stability equal to and even excelling anything heretofore produced. A most wonderful transformation has thus been effected; the phosphate baking powder, once the most unstable, now being the most stable powder on the market. This result presents but another illustration of what patient, determined research may accomplish in overcoming apparently insurmountable obstacles.

Valuation of Baking Powders.

From our observations of the practical operation of Baking Powders, three questions present themselves for consideration in their quantitative valuation.

First,—The total carbon dioxide available in the baking process.

Second,—The conditions under which evolution of the carbon dioxide takes place.

Third,—The keeping quality, i. e., the power of resistance to deteriorating atmospheric influence.

The first two may be referred to an arbitrary standard; while the third must be, from the very nature of the case, purely relative.

Total available Carbon Dioxide.

Weigh out 5 grams of sample into the evolving bottle A of my volumetric carbon dioxide apparatus, for description of which see context, and determine the total carbon dioxide by evolution with acid as therein described. Or the total carbon dioxide may be determined by any other reliable method. For this work, however, my apparatus possesses special advantages in rapidity and accuracy.

Weigh into a 200 cc. flask, or one of any convenient capacity, 2 grammes of sample, add thereto 20 cc. of water, and heat to rapid boiling for one minute; while yet hot, aspirate the flask, until all gaseous carbon dioxide is removed; then attach to a soda-lime tube, or other form of absorption apparatus, (for convenient arrangement of absorption apparatus see context,) and liberating it from the residue in the flask by use of acid, observing all the well known precautions necessary, determine the carbon dioxide therein. This gives the excess of carbon dioxide remaining in the sample after reaction *per se*. Deducting this excess carbon dioxide from the total carbon dioxide obtained, gives available carbon dioxide in the sample.

For consideration of the amount of water to be employed, and the application of heat to imitate the baking process, see article upon "Commercial Valuation of Cream of Tartar Substitutes" by Charles A. Catlin, Journal of Analytical Chemistry, Vol. IV, page 361, 1890, the essential features of which we have already discussed. (See page 12.)

It is preferable to determine total carbon dioxide and excess carbon dioxide, and by difference obtain available carbon dioxide; than to determine available carbon dioxide directly; because of the difficulties of evolution and absorption encountered in the latter method.

These give percentage by weight. Since, however, baking powders are never used by weight, but always by measure (volume), an important factor is to obtain the gravimetric-density of the sample; that is, its commercial volume; and from this to calculate its total volumetric leavening or aerating coefficient. Of course, one may obtain the density of the powder by any of the well known methods; but the exact commercial condition in which it reaches the consumer, is more nearly arrived at by measurement of the contents in the package when opened. For instance, the space occupied by the powder in a can as received, is easily determined; this taken with the total weight of contents gives data for arriving at commercial density.

Thus we get weight of a cubic inch of powder in commercial condition, and, from analysis obtained, calculate to cubic inches its carbon dioxide at 0^0 C. and normal pressure (760 m m). · Suppose we get in this way 50 cubic inches of gas; we would then have a volumetric leavening (aerating) coefficient of 50. This then means, that a given volume of the sample of baking powder will yield in the baking process, 50 times its volume of leavening gas. This is a very important question to be considered; as it is readily seen, that as much actual leavening value may be obtained in domestic use from a powder having low percentage of carbon dioxide with high density, as from one having high percentage carbon dioxide with low density. Therefore, the true measure of efficiency is not one of weight percentage carbon dioxide, as is usually reported, but one of volume evolution.

Conditions under which Carbon Dioxide is Evolved.

Weigh 5 grammes of the sample into the evolving bottle A, of my volumetric carbon dioxide apparatus, using 50 cc. of water in place of the acid as described, and determine at normal temperature the carbon dioxide evolved after twenty minutes of reaction. This gives the so-called cold strength of the sample, serving as an approximate measure of the aerating power outside the oven. Burnt alum powders, for instance, under these conditions, give but little; while those made from free tartaric acid evolve nearly all their available gas.·

The ratio between the total available, and the cold available carbon dioxide, is a matter of careful adjustment in skilled manufacture; and effort is made to bring it to the point of greatest efficiency. It is readily understood that a powder evolving all its available gas in the cold, presents great opportunity for excessive loss of leavening power during the mixing of the dough, with disastrous results in the finished product; while one so tardy in its action as to require the heat of the oven to excite it, can produce nothing but disappointing results, the leavening gas escaping from the cracks of the crusted dough without producing the desired cellular condition.

Keeping Quality.

Atmospheric moisture is the deteriorating agent assailing baking powders. From the very nature of their composition, all are susceptible to its influence in a greater or less degree. The measure of resistance to this influence, of any sample, must therefore be purely relative. It is obtained by exposing a series of samples under consideration, to the influence of an artificially moistened atmosphere produced in a bell glass over water. Exposure to such an atmosphere, of course, is an extreme test, since it is saturated with moisture; a condition rarely if ever encountered in commercial exposure.

First, in each of the thoroughly mixed samples, the total carbon dioxide content is determined, preferably in my volumetric carbon dioxide apparatus; then a series of 5 gram charges are weighed up from each sample and placed upon watch glasses. A wire net being fixed over the water under the bell glass, but not touching it, these watch glasses with their contents are placed upon it (all under the same bell glass), and kept there for the length of time the exposure is desired. At the end of the exposure they are removed, and the total carbon dioxide content determined in each, in my volumetric apparatus, or by other means. The difference between the total carbon dioxide at start and the total carbon dioxide in the charge after exposure, represents the relative loss for each sample under the same condition. This loss calculated into per cent. upon the total carbon dioxide at the start, of course gives fair measure for comparison. To illustrate: Suppose we have three samples of baking powder we wish to compare as to keeping quality, A, B and C, through periods of ten, twenty and thirty hours of the moist air exposure. We first determine the total carbon dioxide percentage in each; then weigh out on watch glasses three charges of 5 grammes each from sample A, marking them A^1, A^2 and A^3; from sample B three charges of like weight each, marking them B^1, B^2 and B^3; and the same from sample C, marking them C^1, C^2 and C^3. All of these nine samples are placed at the same time in the same saturated atmosphere under the bell glass, and the time noted. After ten hours, charges A^1, B^1 and C^1 are removed and their carbon dioxide contents determined.   After twenty hours total exposure, charges A², B² and C² are removed and their carbon dioxide contents determined.   And after thirty hours total exposure, charges A³, B³ and C³ are likewise removed and carbon dioxide contents determined. Any convenient number of samples may be carried through in series, and any desired length of exposure adopted.   Finally the carbon dioxide loss calculated into per cent. of carbon dioxide at start, gives the basis for comparison.   In this manner the relative keeping quality may be determined between samples of baking powders; and experience has shown that the results obtained accord with atmospheric exposures.

LIBRARY
OF THE
UNIVERSITY
OF CALIFORNIA

Fig. 1.   Front view.

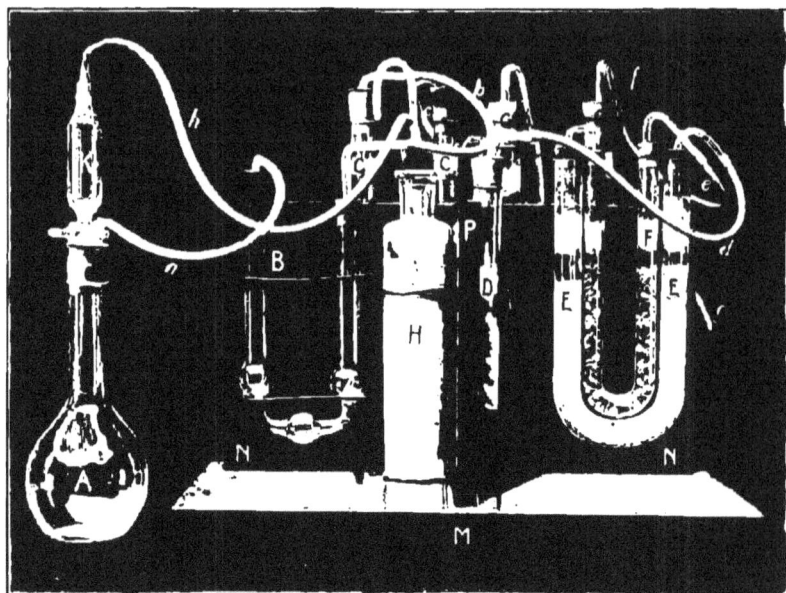

Fig. 2.   Back view.

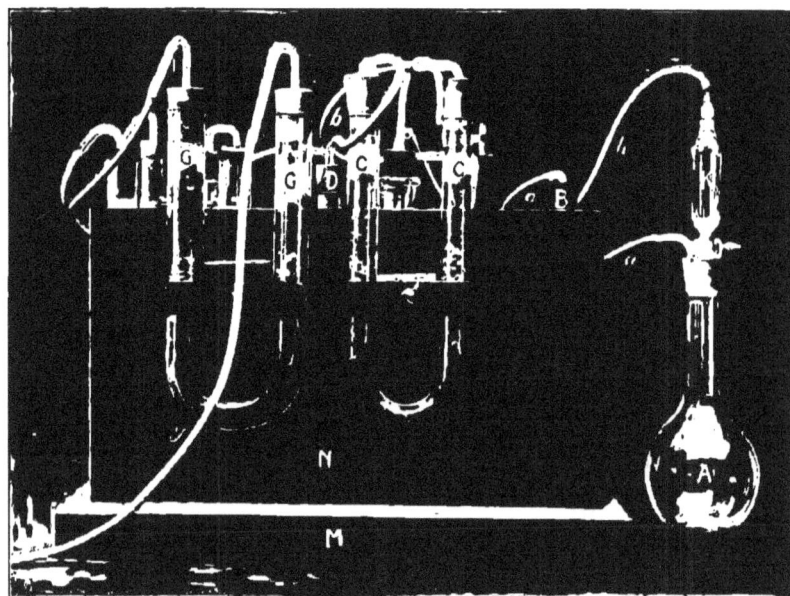

Absorption Apparatus, used in the Rumford Laboratory for the gravimetric determination of carbon dioxide.

Carbon Dioxide Absorption Apparatus.

A convenient and compact arrangement for a carbon dioxide absorption apparatus which I have devised, may be described as follows, reference being had to the accompanying cuts, Fig. 1 showing a front view, Fig. 2 a back view:

Upon the base M is fixed the longitudinal upright N, and about midway of this, the transverse upright P, these to support and hold in position the U-tubes, etc. forming the essential parts.   A is the generating flask of convenient capacity, K a reservoir for the decomposing acid with tube running to the bottom of A, connecting through *h* with the catch bottle H containing soda-lime, to retain any atmospheric carbon dioxide when air is aspirated through it.   B is a small bulb U-tube fixed upon the front side of the longitudinal upright at its left hand end, containing concentrated sulphuric acid, connecting at one limb with the exit tube *a* of the flask A and at the other limb with the tube *b*. C is a plain U-tube fixed upon the back of the upright N, as shown in Fig. 2, connecting with B by tube *b*, containing pumice stone saturated with concentrated sulphuric acid.   D is a plain U-tube fixed upon the transverse upright P, connecting with C by *c*, containing pumice stone treated with cupric sulphate, as a catch

29

tube for hydrochloric acid. E is the soda-lime absorption U-tube connected with D by *d*. F is the drying
tube containing pumice stone saturated with concentrated sulphuric acid, connected directly with E. E and
F together, with the tube *d* forming the parts to be
weighed. G is a plain U-tube fixed upon the back of
the upright N, as shown in Fig. 2, connecting with F
by the tube *e*, containing pumice stone saturated with
concentrated sulphuric acid, serving as a catch tube for
any atmospheric moisture which otherwise might retreat
into the tubes E and F. *g* connects G with an aspirator. *f* is a wire loop suspending the couplet E and
F upon the hook as shown.

The method of operating this apparatus is as follows:

The absorption couplet E F being detached by
drawing off the tube *d* from D, and *e* from F, and
connecting *d* with F, is thus completely sealed from
absorption from the air. In this condition the weight
of E F *d* is carefully obtained by suspending from the
pan hook of the balance by the wire loop *f*. When
the weight is obtained, the couplet is re-attached to the
apparatus in its former position. The weighed charge
of the material in which the carbon dioxide is to be
determined, having been introduced into the flask A and
the requisite amount of decomposing acid into K with
the stopcock closed, the whole apparatus is connected
as shown in the cut. The aspirator being set in operation, the stopcock of K is opened and the acid allowed
to flow down into A, the aspirating air current flowing
along first through soda-lime bottle H, to remove all
atmospheric carbon dioxide, thence through *h*, K, A,

a, B, *b*, C, *c*, D, *d*, E, F, *e*, G, *g*. The stopcock of K
being now closed, heat is applied to the flask A and
its contents brought to a rapid boil continued for a few
minutes. The tube *h* now being disconnected from H
is dipped into a quantity of boiling water and the stopcock of K opened again, when the flask A is allowed
to completely fill with the hot water, up and into the
elbow of the glass tube, where the rubber tube *h* is
attached. In this manner the atmosphere of A is at
once displaced and much time saved in unnecessary
aspiration. The rubber tube *a*, being pinched meanwhile, is drawn off from A and affixed to H, which
thus cuts out A and its attachments, and leaves the
course of the aspirating current to flow through H,
a, B, *b*, C, *c*, D, *d*, E, F, *e*, G, *g*, the carbon dioxide
being quickly swept through the series and absorbed
by the soda-lime of E. The current of pure air may
be drawn through the apparatus at this stage with considerable rapidity; at the rate of four or five litres at
least, within ten minutes, without fear of error; which
would not be the case had the flask A with its steaming
contents remained in the circuit, when certainly, in such
rapid flow, some moisture would have been carried
beyond B, C and D into the absorption couplet. The
concentrated sulphuric acid in B should be changed
with almost every determination, thus maintaining C
for a long time in efficient condition. The effect
of boiling A is of course to heat up the contents
of B, which is desirable; for, while concentrated
sulphuric acid has but slight cold absorption for carbon
dioxide, it nevertheless would absorb a trace, giving

error to that extent, which might be appreciable should excessive sulphuric acid be used. Allowing the sulphuric acid in B to heat up slightly, prevents absorption of any carbon dioxide therein, yet forming an efficient trap for moisture. Of course the sulphuric acid used in the other drying tubes of the apparatus would have this property of slight absorption of carbon dioxide and introduce a source of error, were it not, that, by allowing a current of dry carbon dioxide to flow through these drying tubes for a few moments, previous to using for the first time, (of course not through the absorption tube,) and then aspirating with pure air before actual use, the sulphuric acid is saturated and error from this source avoided. This apparatus furnishes a rapid and accurate means for determining carbon dioxide by absorption.

LIBRARY
OF THE
UNIVERSITY
OF CALIFORNIA

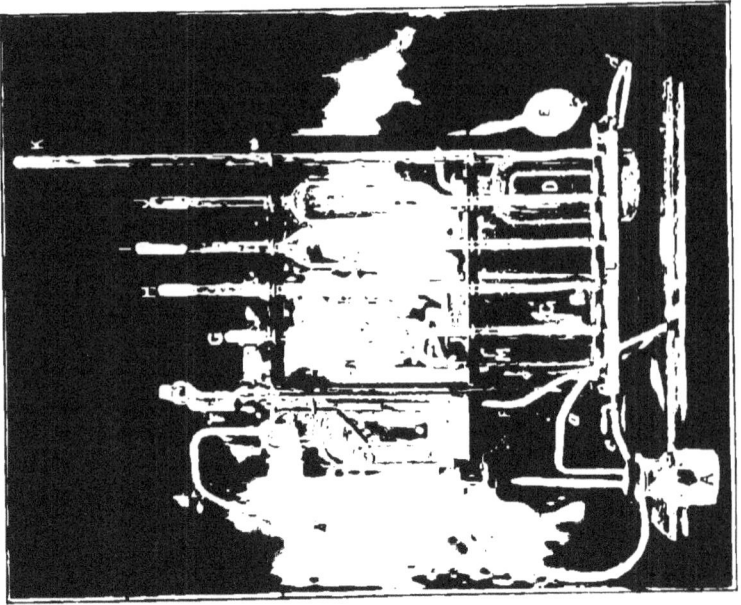

Improved apparatus for the volumetric determination of Carbon Dioxide and other gases. [1]

For the determination of small quantities of carbon dioxide in readily decomposed carbonates, the process and apparatus devised by Dr. Scheibler presents a most convenient and rapid method; but the inability to thus measure large quantities of gas has restricted its employment for the most part to determination of carbonate in bone-char. To extend the field of volumetric carbon dioxide determination I have devised the following described apparatus, retaining, as far as possible, the essential features of the Scheibler.

Referring to the cut: A, C and D are essentially the same as in the Scheibler apparatus; A being the decomposing bottle in which the portion of the sample to be operated upon, is placed, with its enclosed tube for the decomposing acid or other solution, with the further addition however, of a thermometer, inserted through the rubber stopper—a most important feature when the decomposition results in wide variations of temperature; C the bottle containing the rubber gas balloon connected with A; and D the water reservoir with compressing-bulb E, exactly as in the Scheibler device. In the Scheibler apparatus, however, the gas evolved is directly determined by the displacement of water in a graduated tube, the capacity of which is, and must be, quite limited.

[1] Journal of the American Chemical Society, 1893, page 614.

35

In my apparatus I have replaced this graduated tube by the bottle B, connected by the tube *b* with the space around the rubber bag in the bottle C, and by the tube *c*, from its bottom, through the stopcock, with the tube L; which tube L connects, through another stopcock at its opposite end, with the reservoir D, by means of the tube *d*. This tube L, which may be constructed of brass if more convenient, is fixed horizontally upon the standards, as shown in the cut, and has affixed along its upper portion, a series of stopcocks, one of which connects with the tube F, and each of the others individually, with the pipettes G, H, I and J, and the burette K. These pipettes may be respectively (using a fifty cc. burette for K) 50, 100, 200 and 200 cc. capacity, graduated as to contents, between marks on the stem and delivery tube, in each case. The tube F serves as an equalizer of pressure, as hereinafter described.   N shows a common tube thermometer attached to the standard for convenient reference.

Before using the apparatus, the reservoir D is supplied with water, and by means of the compressing-bulb E, the burette and pipettes are filled to their zero marks, and their respective stopcocks closed, the stopcocks connecting *c* and F being closed meanwhile. The stopcock connecting *c* is now opened, and the bottle B filled a little above a zero mark upon the tube *b*, which for a portion of the way is of glass; this glass tube being so inserted in the rubber stopper that the bottle may be entirely filled with water without air space.   During the filling of B, the stopcock M should be opened, connecting as it does with the air space surrounding the gas bag within the bottle C, while the generating bottle A should be disconnected and the gas bag collapsed.   When B is filled, the stop-cock connecting it with L is closed, and that at F opened, and this tube filled in like manner to a point higher than the zero mark of B, when the stopcock connecting d is closed, and that at c opened again. The generating bottle A with its charge of sample and acid in the tube, is now connected, and through the stopcock connecting d the level of the water in B adjusted to the zero mark, that in F subsiding with it.[2] When the adjustment is thus effected, the stopcocks connecting F, and that at M are closed, while that connecting with the reservoir through d, is opened, and thus free course given for the water between B and D. The bottle B being elevated upon the shelf O, there is of course a reduction of pressure within the apparatus, caused by subsidence of the water level; which after a few moments should cease, showing that the apparatus is tight in every joint.   If, however, this is not the case, and the level continues to subside, there is a leak, which must be stopped and a readjustment of pressure effected before the operation is continued.

When all is in readiness, the decomposition of the carbonate is effected in A by bringing the acid and carbonate together in the usual way, the temperature having been noted at the outset.   The evolution of the gas, distending the rubber gas bag, expels a portion of the air from C, which forces the water from B into the

---

[2] Experience in operating this apparatus has shown that it is desirable to attach a U-tube manometer to a branch placed in tube a, near its connection with the rubber bag in C, for the more accurate adjustment of the gas to atmospheric pressure.

reservoir D, in volume equivalent to the gas evolved at
the pressure and temperature prevailing, as is readily
understood. When complete decomposition is effected,
and the temperature in A returns to the temperature of
the room, by means of the bulb E, pressure is exerted
upon the reservoir D, and the stopcock connecting F
being opened, the levels in B and F are brought together
through the stopcock connecting d.

When this is accomplished, the stopcock at F and d
are closed. It is seen that the displacement of the
water in B, obtained in this manner is exactly that of
the volume of the gas evolved from the carbonate at
the existing temperature and atmospheric pressure.
With all stopcocks closed, excepting that connecting
c, and that at M which should now be opened, the
bottle B is removed from its shelf to the table upon
which the apparatus stands, and the amount of the
displacement measured by running in the contents of
such of the pipettes, and portion of the contents of the
burette, as may be required to restore the water level
in B to the starting point, the amount of water thus
employed of course being that measure.

From the volume of gas obtained, the percentage by
weight of the sample taken is calculated in the usual
way, either by the formula for correction of volume
for temperature and pressure, adding of course to the
volume thus obtained a correction for carbon dioxide
dissolved in the decomposing liquid, or through the use
of the tables given originally by Dietrich, (Ztschr.
anal. Chem., 4, 141). It is to be noted, however, that
these tables are not strictly correct, the weight of the

cubic centimeter of carbon dioxide at O^0 C. 760 mgms. being considerably at variance with that at present given by the best authorities; and some slight errors, in the calculation apparently, are also to be observed. In ordinary work, however, these are not important. But in the use of the table given for solubility of the gas in the decomposing acid, one must exercise no little caution. In fact for this correction, it is better to establish for one's self just what it should be for each material operated upon, by check gravimetric determinations; for while within limits, this may be taken as a constant factor, yet it is more or less affected by the character of the salts present. And further, this table was not carried far enough to cover the large volumes of gas evolved from the charges that my apparatus enables one to employ.

With this apparatus it is possible to make a determination of carbon dioxide in from ten to fifteen minutes, and that with extreme accuracy. Indeed with the large charges one may employ, and with careful weighings, repeated results obtained from the same sample will never vary more than one-tenth per cent. and scarcely more in most instances than two or three one-hundredths per cent.

For some operations, more particularly where the carbon dioxide evolved by cold water is to be determined in a baking powder, I have devised the fittings and arrangement of the decomposing bottle A, as shown in the accompanying cut.

A third hole is pierced through the stopper of A, through which is introduced the stem of the glass-stoppered funnel tube P, bearing the stopcock r, and having, from its upper portion, the air tube S, connecting with a branch inserted in the tube a. It is readily seen

from this, that the weighed charge may be placed in A, the
stopper inserted, and, with the stopcock *r* closed, the charge of
decomposing liquid placed in P, and the stopper of P also inserted,
when connection may be made with the rest of the apparatus at
a.   All being ready, by opening the stopcock *r*, the liquid flows
readily into A, the necessary air displacement taking place
through S, the rest of the operation being conducted as above
described.

www.ingramcontent.com/pod-product-compliance
Lightning Source LLC
Chambersburg PA
CBHW032140080426
42733CB00008B/1143